GIRLFRIEND VS. WIFE DUTIES

BY DARSHAUN MCAWAY

God is my strength and my source without him nothing will be.

Do, or do not. There is no "try."

Email: darshaun@darshaun.com
URL: http://www.darshaun.com

Original illustrations / Photographs by Darshaun McAway
Printed by www.Darshaun.com and Lulu Press
Girlfriend vs. Wife Duties by Darshaun Mcaway
Publisher: Darshaun McAway
Proofreader: Sable Stubbs
Editing: Sara Madeline Hopkins

ISBN: 978-0-578-11847-5

<u>Acknowledgements</u>

I would like to express my gratitude to the many people who saw me through this book; to all those who provided support, talked things over, read, wrote, offered comments, allowed me to quote their remarks and assisted in the editing, proofreading, and design. I would like to thank God for enabling me to publish this book. Above all I want to thank my mom, and the rest of my family, who supported and encouraged me in spite of all the time it took me away from them. It was a long and difficult journey for them.

I would like to thank Angelina Smith, Lasharna Brooks, for inspiring me to write this book. Thanks to Henri McQueen who encouraged me for many years to just keep writing. Thanks to Rachel Rushefsky and Sara Madeline Hopkins—without you this book would never find its way to the Web. Last and not least: I beg forgiveness of all those who have been with me over the course of the years and whose names I have failed to mention.

Prologue

*By humility and the fear of the Lord are
riches, and honor, and life.*

—Proverbs 22:4

Table of Contents

Lesson 1

Take Care Of Your Man!!!

A woman accompanied her husband to the doctor's office. After his checkup, the doctor called the wife into his office alone. He said, "Your husband is suffering from a very severe disease, combined with horrible stress. If you don't do the following, your husband will surely die: Each morning, fix him a healthy breakfast. Be pleasant, and make sure he is in a good mood. For lunch make him a nutritious meal he can take to work. And for dinner, prepare an especially nice meal for him. Don't burden him with chores, as this could increase his stress. Don't discuss your problems with him; it will only make his stress worse.

"Try to relax your husband in the evening by wearing lingerie and giving him plenty of back rubs. Encourage him to watch some type of team sporting event on television. And, most importantly, make love with your husband several times a week and satisfy his every whim. If you can do this for the next ten months to a year, I think your husband will regain his health completely."

On the way home, the husband asked his wife, "What did the doctor say?"

She replied, "Your disease is terminal, you're going to die."

Introduction

This book is about accomplishing your goals before you get married. When you apply for a job, always make sure you read the job description:

JOB TITLE: WIFE

Reports to: Husband
Based at: Your Sparkly Home, Your House, Your World

JOB DESCRIPTION
Responsible for all household and childcare duties

Additionally, the housewife is responsible for ensuring that harmony exists between all individuals living in the home. Love, care, and kindness are all attributes that must be exhibited by the housewife. Caring for the husband is crucial, and it is expected that the housewife will provide for his emotional, physical, and spiritual needs. A housewife should also maintain good personal hygiene, a healthy diet, and exercise regularly.

While there is not a strict dress code, it is expected that between the hours of 7 a.m. and 10 p.m., the housewife will have makeup applied and will not be wearing pajamas or other elastic clothing. The housewife is expected to maintain a tranquil demeanor and a calm voice.

DUTIES
Household:
- *Sweeping/Mopping* – at least once per day
- *Dusting* – at least twice per week
- *Vacuuming* – at least once per week
- *Straightening Up* – at least once per day, preferably before 5 p.m.
- *Tidying the Kitchen* – as often as needed so that dishes do not extend over the corners of the sink
- *Scrubbing Bathrooms* – at least once every two weeks or weekly if young children reside in the home

- *Doing the Laundry* – as often as necessary so that clean socks and underwear can easily be located
- *Other Duties* – as needed

Childcare:
- *Feeding* – 3 well balanced meals each day with 1-2 healthy snacks
- *Bathing* – at least 3 baths per week including full body lotion application as needed
- *Dressing/Grooming* – children will be dressed by 8 a.m. in fresh, clean clothes. Haircuts must be provided every 6 weeks once the child is 18 months old. Fingernails and toenails must be trimmed so that no part of the nail extends past the end of the finger.
- *Developmental* – reading to each child for at least 20 minutes every day
- *Emotional Caring* – holding each child for at least 20 minutes per day. Saying "I love you" to each child at least 3 times a day.

QUALIFICATIONS/REQUIREMENTS:
- Must have a high threshold for pain and a high tolerance

for nagging, bothering, begging, crying, and loud noises

☐ Must be willing and able to stand for extended periods of time, to crawl on the floor, to enter tight and cramped spaces, and to climb on chairs and tables to obtain objects in difficult-to-reach places

☐ Must be willing and able to operate on 4-6 hours of sleep, usually interrupted

☐ Should be able to handle multiple difficult situations at once

☐ Should be well versed in phone etiquette and possess writing skills

☐ Must negotiate requests from both children and adults

☐ Must calmly handle stressful situations without yelling, throwing, hitting, storming out of rooms, or slamming doors - preferably

Anything else I'm missing?

Now when you apply for any job you always read the description because it explains your duties to the employer and you don't accept the job unless you know you can handle it. When the employer hires you and you start work, the first two weeks they don't expect much because you're still in the learning phase and working out the kinks. However, when the third week begins, they expect for you to perform the duties they hired you for.

What am I saying? In relationships it works the same way, after you date someone for a few days, weeks, or months, you start to interview the candidates you have an interest in and who suit your needs. Perhaps you would like to hire that special person into your life to perform certain duties. And I notice, once you hire that person, the first couple of weeks or maybe even months you let a few things slide; but after a while you start to implement an action plan to get this person to fulfill the job description that you hired them for.

But then all of a sudden they're getting comfortable with the job. They start showing up late, leaving early, and getting away with doing no work while you're investing money, time, and emotion in someone who's not doing the "job." You're realizing that your time and effort are being wasted and maybe you hired the wrong person. That's what this book is about: hiring, or should I say *allowing,* the wrong person into your life because you didn't pay attention to the small details they informed you about early on.

Now with that being said, I would never put any more responsibility on a person who considers it a burden to work at our relationship. The last thing I need is for someone to be with me who doesn't feel like they have to do anything—and when I say anything, I mean *anything.*

Girlfriend vs. Wife Duties. I hope you enjoy the book, I had a lot of fun putting it together.

Chapter 1

What Separates a Girlfriend from a Wife?

Besides the Ring.

Before you learn about a relationship, what do you know about yourself?

Now, ladies, before I answer the question that every woman on the face of the planet wants to ask, I want to get into why most women are girlfriends for an extremely long time. I'm talking about years. One of the main reasons that you are not his wife will always be that you're not meeting his preferred needs in the first place. I wish I could say it's about you having sex too soon, but adults having consensual sex doesn't determine whether or not he will marry you later on. It's the performance, character, and personality that determines the length of the courtship and the commitment you have for one another. I say that because there are thousands of success stories about people having sex in the beginning and later getting married and staying married.

It's safe to say that as a girlfriend it is your priority to take care of *your* individual needs, wants, and responsibilities (while showing your boyfriend that you have his best interests at heart should he decide to take your hand in marriage) and for your boyfriend to solely take care of *his* needs, wants, etc. (while keeping *your* best interests at heart). You see, as boyfriend and girlfriend the overall goal is to be joined as husband and wife, but before you tie any knots together, you first have to learn how to take care of your own life, hence the truism "take your time and be friends."

However, most of us jump the gun and get into a relationship that we can't handle. It makes sense to become established in your life rather than getting into someone else's life and then trying to figure out how and where to go next, or even getting into a relationship thinking only, "What's in it for me?" The most common misconception is that you can change, make, or eventually coerce another person to come around to your needs and wants. With this type of thinking you're all out of focus. Instead, you have to learn to be just like the title says, a girlfriend vs. a wife, or else you'll find yourself failing at a job that you didn't apply for because you don't know the requirements. Most women aren't born with the skill set to be a wife. Therefore it's necessary to learn about yourself before you wander off thinking, *I have what every man wants*. Relationships are like jobs, you have to constantly do the best you can to keep the position.

Developing into a wife takes more than feeling that you're a good woman with good intentions. It's about commitment, dedication, and laying your wants and needs aside for the betterment of your man and your family. Everyone's point of view on relationships is different, so I wanted to make sure that with this book I focus on why girlfriends are doing what wives do without actually having the title of wife.

Now to give the answer that every woman wants to know. What separates a girlfriend from a wife is that a wife is very careful to recommend herself to her husband's esteem and affection, to know his mind, and is willing that he rule over her. She can be trusted, and he will leave such a wife to manage for him. He is happy in her. And she makes it her constant business to do him good. She is one that takes pains in her duties, and takes pleasure in them. She is careful to fill up her time, that none be lost. She applies herself to the business proper for her, to women's business. She does what she does, with all her power, and trifles not. She makes what she does turn to good account by prudent management. Many undo themselves by buying, without considering what they can afford. A wife provides well for her house. She lays up for hereafter. She looks well to the ways of her household, that she may oblige all to do their duty to God and one another, as well as to her. She is as intent upon giving as upon getting, and does it freely and cheerfully. She is discreet and obliging; every word she says shows she governs herself by the rules of wisdom. She not only takes prudent measures herself, but gives prudent advice to others. The law of love and kindness is written in the heart, and shows itself in the tongue. Her heart is full of another world, even when her hands are most busy about this world. Above all, she fears the Lord.

Beauty recommends none to God, nor is it any proof of wisdom and goodness, but it has deceived many a man who made his choice of a wife by it. But the fear of God reigning in the heart is the beauty of the soul; it lasts forever.

She has firmness to bear up under crosses and disappointments. She shall reflect with comfort when she comes to be old that she was not idle or useless when young. She shall rejoice in a world to come. She is a great blessing to her relations. If the fruit be good, the tree must have our good word. But she is not boastful and leaves it to her own works to praise her. Everyone ought to desire this honor that cometh from God; and according to this standard we all ought to regulate our judgments. This description let all women who desire to be respected, useful, and honorable study daily.

Understanding what this means and living it is what will develop you into a wife; while a girlfriend strives to be those things without having the unqualified respect of a man. So by all means continue to be a girlfriend—just don't end up doing the duties of a wife.

Swee'Sarah

Should I just become a wife? I am a girlfriend but my boyfriend and I live together and split bills. I'm a part of his family and we even have twins together. Some people mistake me for a wife, but when I tell them I'm a girlfriend they are shocked.

LavenderpXD

What's the difference?

Sister_Bea

I think you should become his wife, it only makes sense—I mean, c'mon, you've got kids together.

ItCity-Gurl

Stay a girlfriend!!! It's easier and you don't have to worry about legal stuff.

Another thought: he probably hasn't proposed because he's thinking, "If she's not sharing responsibility in the relationship, making any compromises, or even having a full commitment to me...then why should I commit to her?"

Throughout history it's been proven that

everyone needs a helping hand. But what separates a girlfriend from a wife—aside from the fact that you cannot get rid of a wife easily? A girlfriend is an individual that's focused on her life which is why many girlfriends may be vaguely annoying and may be somewhat needy. As for a wife, well, you can instantly tell that she has qualities that are 100 percent unselfish, mature, family driven, and—dare I say it?—submissive. But please keep in mind most women who decide to get married also realize that their husband is submissive to their needs as well. Saying "I do" is saying "hello" to all kinds of comprises. In order to be a wife you have to first give up your independent life and know that you're doing this for the greater good of raising a family and investing a lifetime with a partner that's responsible with money and time, and values life and family. A wife is a woman who has preparation, preservation, and common sense. A husband is a better man with her by his side.

Most men in the boyfriend-and-girlfriend stage want you to be emotionally understanding of their circumstances when it comes to life's trials and tribulations, to understand that they're doing the best they can as a man to provide and show empathy toward you in the struggle as well.

Marriage is ideally supposed to be a shared experience between the spouses. Though, more often, control is lent to the husband. As a result, this may be why many girlfriends are not wives, either they are fearful of possibly being expected to be submissive or they are just NOT going to accept that notion. This is why some see marriage as a wife doing all tasks for her husband, while the husband, shall I say, sits on the throne of control and power.

The most disheartening truth about this "fact" is that many marriages have the spouses level, with equal control and responsibility. Unfortunately, it's one of most persistent myths that many believe, and some even praise the thought of a wife being always submissive with no leniency and with the husband having almost total control. Thus leading to marriages that end before they begin. But you can put someone else's needs first without completely forfeiting your identity.

However, girlfriends are generally less inclined to make a major compromise compared to a wife. Why is this? The answer may well be "Why compromise for a relationship that's not 'complete'?" It is a paradox to "Why buy the cow when you can have free milk?"

And, I honestly believe you can put the "free milk" phrase out there, but it won't change the fact that most men and women will ultimately choose who they want based off potential, growth, and not sex.

-There has to be something about you in order for a man to make you his wife.

-Most of the time the men you meet won't feel like there's anything special about you. A man has to feel like he is willing to do or die for you.

Now, lest I undermine girlfriends, it's important to note that a girlfriend is often a woman in the early stage of what can easily be a transition into a fully committed wife. Imagine it this way, a girlfriend may have a *shaky* time making compromises but has *average* commitment, a fiancée *regularly* makes compromises with *confidence* on commitment, and lastly the *ideal* wife *willingly* makes compromises and has an "until death" commitment.

A girlfriend has a greater possibility of leaving a relationship comfortably. In contrast, the wife may be bound culturally or financially or religiously, because she knew that it was "'til death" and she may go through a lengthy divorce with all the legal drama if the relationship ends.

Chapter 2

Knowing Your Identity

MissLeshe

I really want to know what I am to this guy. We both are attracted to each other and he calls me sometimes to hookup. He tells me that he really loves me and would do anything for me. So what am I to him?

Camron'astro

I think it's safe to say that you're his girlfriend.

CasanovaSuave

Not a mind reader... Ask him.

Noyolo4u

You are...quick-fix girl!!! Nah, just kidding, you're on speed dial for when he gets lonely.

PopC

Well, what do you act like to him?

Please, perform a self-evaluation with this list:

1. Is your boyfriend doing most of the compromising in the relationship?

2. Do you have more control in the relationship and use it on your boyfriend?

3. Is there an unfair burden of responsibility on your boyfriend?

4. Do you break up often?

5. If you break up often, do you find yourself wandering to other people for a relationship or looking for other partners?

6. Do you make few to no compromises that mean anything or affect the relationship?

7. Do you find yourself automatically saying, "I'm not your wife," when he asks for something, whether it be a task, favor, or compromise?

8. Were you unfaithful to the relationship,

i.e., had an affair or lied to your boyfriend?

9. Do you attract a lot of drama?

If you answered yes to any of the questions above, try to work on them until you are able to answer no to them all. Maybe then, he will propose.

Evaluate yourself. Are you just a quick one-hit chick or are you defined in the picture? Look at what you do in the relationship (if there is one) and how it impacts him. Is your role deciding if he gets short-lived satisfaction tonight or if he'll love and respect you forever? Ladies, I am not trying to criticize your particular situation or stance in a relationship, but if you really want to know your identity look at the effects of what you do in the relationship, and the importance and impact of it. As a person do you see yourself as the girlfriend or the wife?

In this new day and age everyone is rushing into these statuses of girlfriend, boo, bust it, baby, side piece, bust down, wife, and only accepting it because you don't care who you are and you're willing to be whatever a guy wants you to be because you want him more than he wants you. Why force yourself to settle, why not set the standard by letting him know you're wife material?

I can't tell you how many times women settle for what they think is the next best thing walking. I've learned that in this life it's about having what you want and not settling for last place, especially if you can change it. Don't find yourself working a job you didn't apply for (and aren't compensated for). You'll be miserable and wondering where you went wrong. Then you'll be stuck in the abyss of figuring out who you are and what's your purpose as a woman.

When women get into a relationship most

men, if not all, will state in the beginning that they want to see you succeed in whatever you want to do; but then sometimes they do not show you they want you to do it, much less succeed. If you've ever experienced this I'm sure you realized that at some point you will settle and compromise with your partner just to avoid or end an argument. However, at some point in time you'll push the issue of pursuing your passions. That's why it's so important to become a friend in the beginning of a potential relationship, so you can continue to push out your dreams and once you decide to take it to the committed level you can incorporate the dreams and goals together to start creating unity within the home you both established.

So at this point you may be thinking, *Well, who am I, and who am I to him?* Where's my value in this thing we call a relationship or marriage. If you have ever asked yourself this, now is the time for you to stop your old habits of settling and start getting out your dreams. As a girlfriend it's so important that you stress to your boyfriend that you're not his task manager, washing machine, and—here it goes—his wife. Yup, that's right, you're not his wife. Have you ever wondered why you always hear some women say, "Girl, you're not his wife, I don't know why you doing that"? They make a valid point. You, young lady, are his girlfriend and until both of you decide to get it together things will have to remain apart. Why? Because neither of you are ready for marriage. And if neither of you understand the difference between girlfriend and wife, how can you move from dating to marriage?

Do you know how important it is to show and prove to a man that you're willing to be taken care of throughout life? Honestly, think about it. Men have the stigma of being head of the household, and just because you think you look good, smell nice, or have your head on straight doesn't mean you're the one he wants to take care of for the rest of his life. Take away the fact that he's a man for a second and get rid of the men vs. women and let's focus on solely taking care of a **person**. Now let's look into what type of person you're taking care of. Are they lovable, annoying, a joy to be around, depressing to be around, do they have social intellect, are they grateful when you do something for them genuinely? Nine times out of ten they have two traits that you value and that is that they are lovable and a joy to be around most of the time. Now multiply that times ten and for the rest of your life with children. If a person can love you through all your flaws that's one hell of a person to marry. And I'm more than sure he has some issues in his life too and he's expecting you to love him through his flaws as well.

So let's recap just a little bit. Know your identity needs to be developed before you even get into a relationship. Why?

Because you need to show him that you're worth his entire time. He needs to see how you value yourself and how you treat yourself. Anytime throughout life when you hear, or overhear, gossip dealing with another couple, no one really values the other person. They just hooked up and went from there. A man will pretty much treat you the way he sees you treating yourself. If you're looking for yourself, well, he'll be looking for other options until you find yourself. Therefore you'll always be girlfriend material or whatever you labeled the relationship to be. Take ownership and stop settling for anything that comes your way. It doesn't matter if you're a single parent with four kids, you can still be a wife, but you have to prove it. I'm sure you don't like the thought of proving anything to anyone but every woman at some point in life will have to prove to some man that they are worth it.

Let's switch gears and say you are the

person that knows yourself and you treat yourself like a queen but you still don't have the title of wife or most men keep treating you like second best. Well, let's figure out why. What are you showing him that you don't show yourself? There has to be something up with you if you've been with a guy for years and he hasn't made you his wife. Always look at your core values; personality has a lot to do with finding the right man. Most likely you have traits that are difficult to be around. Which is why you keep telling yourself, *I don't need a man,* and, *I love being single,* and, *That's fine, because being a wife is a "lifestyle choice" and not a "requirement."* Therefore, being single is a "lifestyle choice" and not a "default position." It is possible to CHOOSE to be single. There are advantages to being married just as there are disadvantages to being married, such as loss of personal freedom, having to compromise, etc. Conversely, there are advantages to being single, as well as disadvantages. Whether one is married or single is nothing more than a lifestyle choice. Assuming you actively chose it.

Appreciate the absence of compromise. Classic relationship advice dictates that compromise and sacrifice are essential to a healthy relationship. Perhaps if you've been in a relationship before, you realize how much stuff you had to give up in order to make that relationship work. Or maybe you forgot about that stuff, because you're focused on the things you miss. Well, this is a good time to shift that focus. If you're a slob, isn't it great to be able to leave your stuff lying around, without anybody minding? Or if you're a neat freak, isn't it wonderful to be able to organize everything, and find it the way you left it? Isn't it nice to be able to cook and enjoy foods that a partner might be averse to? Isn't it cool to be able to go out spontaneously, without wondering whether your partner can or should be invited? A relationship can add many good things to your life, but it also adds some rigidity, so take the time to appreciate your current flexibility.

Really, do you think of yourself as a girlfriend or a wife, and does he think of you the same way? You obviously can't seriously think of yourself as his wife if he only needs you for a "quick fix." Now, if you handle an equal amount of work, help financially, and live your life with your boyfriend as one person, then, yes, you are basically a wife...without certification.

One major difference between being a girlfriend or a wife is whether you live your lives fairly independently from each other or if your lives are in total sync, being basically one person.

Do not forget, your opinion on your title is null and void if it doesn't match your boyfriend's opinion. Why? Yes, it's your title, but if you look deep, it's your title of your association to him, it's what you are to him.

To assert your identity you need to focus on what you want to be in his view, and if you keep working on that role, he will eventually accept you as you have portrayed yourself.

If you have a relationship based on lust and attraction you really can't call yourself a wife. *If you want to play a role you have to act the part.* Honestly, you can't audition for the role of wife if you portray yourself as largely individual from your partner's life with a relationship centered on attraction and minimal commitment. What you do in the relationship and how you do it will ultimately define your role.

A commitment leads to a building of trust and reliability. Attraction can help keep romance alive. Balancing duties can prevent lopsided burdens. Being prominent and intermingled in your partner's life can ensure understanding and closeness. The amount of these components in a relationship: commitment, attraction, romance, balance, and intermingling, corresponds to your role in the view of your partner. Consider it this way: If you had a man who gave you all his commitment, gave you romance, and was active in your life, you would probably view him as a husband.

Chapter 3

Don't Forget Your Duty

du·ty [doo-tee] Noun, plural *du·ties.*

1. Something that one is expected or required to do by moral or legal obligation.

anna46

Okay, so lately my boyfriend has been asking me to like clean around the house and cook for him. I get that he works and pays the bills and all, but seriously I'm not his wife. Our romance is okay and I spend time with him so why should I clean and cook for him?

Married4-7yrs

@*anna46* I don't think he's trying to burden you, but trying to get you to contribute around the house. He does pay bills, it's only fair.

Gary'sGirl

@*anna46* Sounds like you just need to do those things to relieve the stress on your bf.

anna46

Well, why can't he just accept love? Why he need a

housekeeper?

Married4-7yrs

Girlfriends have responsibilities too and love alone can't help with work. Besides, the less time he has to spend on chores, the more time he can spend with you.

Honestly it depends on the two individuals and how they define their roles. Culture also comes into play here. Whether your role is some stereotypical version of "in-the-kitchen-making-a-sandwich" rude or you are the breadwinner in the house is up to you and your man.

A wife's sense of duty is very dependent on upbringing, cultural influences, and religion. For example, if a woman was raised in a household where her mother stayed home with the kids while the father worked she may assume this type of role in the future, as she may view it as being normal and ideal, or she may view it negatively and actively seek to avoid the role, all depending on if the preceding marriage was successful or chaotic.

If in popular culture the ideal wife cooks, cleans, and earns money to contribute to bills, this is what a woman may strive for in order to be seen as a model wife.

Think about it, in the 1950's in America, TV shows advertised what a wife should be like. Carol Brady, from the *Brady Bunch*, was seen as the "perfect" wife, and Lucy, from *I Love Lucy*, was perceived as a mischievous wife, but still lovable and caring. The effect? A whole mass of women rushed to assume the roles of these "ideal" wives and thus spurred a new era of the "American Wife."

This is not to say that girlfriends don't have duties either. A girlfriend's most important duty is frequently portrayed by the media as sticking by her boyfriend, but this is also a minimum requirement. Contradictory? Who says so?

Now after studying different cultures one has to notice the drastic differences in each. In Islamic culture, a prospective wife's duty is to remain pure by retaining her virginity. In some Islamic cultures if a husband does not find blood after the first intercourse he has with his wife, which is the usual result of the hymen breaking, his wife may be subject to death, beating, or another punishment. Although some hymens may stretch and not bleed, it is still in custom to look for blood. If all is well, the wife is still subject to all orders her husband gives her, the word of Islam, and in some cases, the husband's family.

Some who read this may think: "That is insane!" To *you* it may be, but in another person's culture it is as normal as day, totally expected, and a part of their upbringing.

And in some cultures, girlfriends don't even exist, as one may be promised to a marriage or arranged in a marriage at their birth. There are even some cases of forced marriage, ranging from as simple as shotgun weddings to marry-or-die.

But in the Western world, there may be times when you and your partner don't agree on what your duties should be. Your man may think you should clean up, cook for him, or even pay the bills. Maybe it's a part of his culture and tradition or he simply wishes to balance out responsibilities. Both the man and the woman must realize that compromises are critical components of relationships and can either solve all problems or toss the relationship into an infernal abyss. Which sounds good?

You should try to aim for stability in the relationship by maintaining balance in all duties. It would be unfair for him to work and pay the bills while you don't even watch the kids. Likewise, it would be unjust for your man to expect you to watch the kids, cook, clean, and work and pay the bills.

I think the most important duty that you have is to keep the equality in the relationship and the mutual attraction. This goes for all. A relationship will spiral out of control without this.

In this most of us are extremely lucky that we can stay with whomever we feel connected to. Think about it for a second. You can easily get a boyfriend, move in with him, and if things don't work out, you can up and leave. No ties, no contract, just living life the way you see fit. Besides you know as well I know that relationships are compromise. It's almost safe to say you either get in where you fit in or move on. However, my goal throughout this book is to help you see your self-worth and how important it is for you to hold a man to his self-worth. I know it's safe to say that most men aren't held accountable for most of their actions. They get away with everything under the sun. Cheating, having babies out of wedlock, not having jobs or even putting any effort into getting a job. It's almost like you're supposed to just accept that life is so hard for him that you have to take care of him because he's a boyfriend. Well, that's only partially true. As a woman you must take care of yourself and if you see that your significant other needs some help, by all means lend a helping hand—just not the entire body.

So here's what I propose to all women. Take a stand and hold men accountable again. There's nothing wrong with a man chasing his dream, but if you have more money than he does that doesn't mean he chases his dreams with your bank account. This is especially true if you're a girlfriend, but don't misunderstand me, this doesn't mean if you're a wife that you lend all your financial support to your husband as well. You lend financial support in moderation. If you don't lend or give in moderation you will go broke and there really won't be any dreams nor a relationship worth saving.

So please, ladies, hold men accountable and make them see your worth by the way you support yourselves and take financial responsibility for your own lives. I can almost guarantee you that not too many men will let you bankrupt them if you decide to chase your dreams, so if they won't go broke for you, don't go broke for them.

Chapter 4

Where You Go Wrong
(Miss Independent)

How can you expect a man to feel like he's worth anything if you don't let him prove his worth? As I have already observed, some men like to prove themselves by showing how well they can provide for you—usually with a show of money and financial ability. Other men like to show their worth by doing simple but heartfelt favors for you, but alas, they are hard to find. Now if you are Miss Independent, you are probably wondering, "How does this apply to me and why does it matter?" Well, think about it, usually when a woman says she's independent she believes she doesn't need any reliance on anybody else for money, happiness, or other things.

So picture this:

You're independent, you don't need anybody else to take care of you, but your man offers to pay for something or do something for you. You may think of him as looking down on you, so you may dismiss him. Yet, here's your man thinking: "She won't let me do anything for her, so... what am I supposed to do?"

So now YOU think. What do you really want from him? It all leads to either love without monetary bounds or just downright sex. Realistically, if you don't let him provide for you, then what is he there for?

To start off, doesn't a relationship involve working cooperatively and supporting each other physically and emotionally? So why aim for the opposite? Stop shooting around the target and hit the bull's-eye.

It's okay to be independent, but to over-protect yourself allows no one to be close to you. It's hard to feel mutual affection when you don't let anyone else provide for you and think they're trying to look down on you. You may not want to rely on everyone for everything and that is understandable, but if you do all there is all by yourself then how can someone prove their worth to you?

Maybe you just want commitment. That's cool. Commitment is an important component to a relationship, but if that's all there is will it really last? What about attraction, mutualism, communication, and compromises?

As stated before, the most important duty is to keep equality and mutual attraction in the relationship; that keeps everything flowing. Another thought, as an independent woman you demand respect, correct? Your partner gives it to you, but do you really return it when he tries to do things for you? It's so important to let a man not only play his role but *be the role.* Throughout history men have been looked upon as sole providers and, depending on who you have a relationship with and how much of a bond you two have, it's important to let him be who he's designed to be and that's a man who is willing to support you with his heart. In this lifetime I want women to stop holding material things over men's heads. It's not about what you can do for me lately. It's about how are you treating me lately. Those types of actions speak louder than words. Things fade away, but memories of love last forever.

So don't be so independent that you let the right person slip away. Do your best to bring out the best in a man. Let him know that you need his help, attention, affection, support. We are human and we need love. Most women love to be Ms. Fix-It while a man sits back and plays the role of backseat driver. No, ladies, men need to step up to the plate and support you at the appropriate times. I'm not sure what type of man you have but I hope you are paying close attention to what type of provider he is for you. Every woman brings out a different side in a man. The way one woman acts will make a man want and do for you in different ways. Don't put him under pressure to do things for you; let his genuine feelings for you come through. I don't believe anyone wants to be the person that does things to show you that they love you or care for you. Hold your own when needed. If he offers, then let him handle things from there. My view on how independent women can change their ways is to disable themselves just a little bit to see if this is the type of man that wants to provide for you in the future. I wonder if any woman knows how it feels to have a man truly love you and care for you like the last person on earth. If you can take your time to get to know a man, I think you'll find it worthwhile; you'll see if he's fit to be a suitable husband.

I know that millions of women feel like every man is supposed to provide for his lady on the initial meet and greet. Especially on dates and just going out doing daily activities, but that's not entirely true. You see, there's a great deal of communication that has to be established up front. I can't warn you enough to establish a financial barrier between you and your man-to-be. All men have budget issues and just because he feels like you're a potential girlfriend doesn't mean he wants to spend or simply do everything for you. Now again this theory is coming from a certain time frame within a relationship. Some couples have money issues for months and even years. As a matter of fact, marriage is a financial issue all across the globe, so do your best to help contribute to the goal of financial freedom and not be a burden. If you know it's something that you want and you have the money to purchase it, don't be selfish and coldhearted and make him get it for you just because. That's not the type of disabling I'm talking about. If you're doing that you're the reason this book was written anyway. You are the problem and the reason why most women who run into a good man find he keeps them in the girlfriend zone. You're not being honest. You'll know how to spot a provider just like he'll know when to pick his wife. Doing things for each other will come naturally and there won't be any evil intentions behind it. So be independent, just make sure you pick the right moment to disable it.

Chapter 5

The Unfair Balance

Shellybean

Why do girlfriends have it easier off? You expect that being a wife you would get all these benefits but girlfriends can do the same thing without having to share everything. What's going on?

Zap!pped

Back in my day, a wife was respected and had all the benefits. Girlfriends were seen as hussies. Where did courting go?

DracZack

Wife is a formal term. You don't need to be married anymore. Get with it. -Se Vamp

MiaG

Girlfriends definitely have it better. All the benefits and none of the hassle.

For girlfriends, how many times did your man ask you to do something and your automatic reply was: "I'm not your wife!" Well first of all, you should be asking *why* you're not his wife. Obviously if that was your reply then you realize it's easier off being a girlfriend...rather than a wife. That means subconsciously you may view being a wife as daunting work with outrageous tasks compared to your current position. You may even be thinking, why move up?

For wives, you know you support your husbands and do things for him that no one else could or would do. Also you may think, why do girlfriends have it easier off? Well, this is because some view the title of girlfriend as less commitment held to a relationship than a wife. Please, by any means do not think you should settle for being a girlfriend but rather realize that a wife holds a very honorable and prestigious title.

Whether you are a wife or a girlfriend your duty can vary. Usually girlfriends can enjoy a minimal involvement in their boyfriend's life, with a relationship held up with attraction, romance, or commitment, most times.

Wives have an attached life with their husbands, like an arm and a shoulder. They are entangled together with the marriage being based on love and willingness in most cases. Their job is to be in their husband's life and work together with them in everything that they do.

Sure, being a girlfriend sounds easier. But, think of it this way: a girlfriend is the main course with wine at no cost. It can't get any better, can it? Wrong, a wife is the dessert that he's been waiting for and saving room for in his stomach. And once he gets that dessert, he will savor every taste, and will probably be detached from the main course he finished. Think about it, you always look forward to dessert the most. Which is more regarded?

That analogy was not to say that girlfriends are of less worth and hardly thought of. They are just one course in "the great meal of life," with the dessert being the final and most cherished course. But doesn't the main course always keep him full?

However, a wife can never be as individual and independent as she was before, due to the complete joining of two lives. Is the compromise fair enough? You tell me, it decides what you'll be. Nowadays, a girlfriend can enjoy the same benefits of being a wife such as splitting the bills, having kids, and mingling with each other's families. This is all without being a "certified wife" or "official wife" but rather being considered a wife. This raises a question, why get married and have to deal with legal issues when you can enjoy the same benefits as a girlfriend? Contradictions all around. Cop-out or common sense?

There's a reason and logic to marriage. I remember reading an article by Maggie Gallagher in which she explained, "Married people are both responsible for and responsible to another human being, and both halves of that dynamic lead the married to live more responsible, fruitful, and satisfying lives. Marriage is a transformative act, changing the way two people look at each other, at the future, and at their roles in society."[1]

Millions of marriages have pitfalls and when you say you want to be someone's wife in a roundabout way, you're also stating you're ready for death. Now I don't mean to be a downer in this chapter but this is the reality in which we live. It's cute and fun being someone's girlfriend but becoming a wife is a serious vow.

Ladies, I know most of you don't want a

---

[1] Maggie Gallagher, "Why Marriage Is Good for You," *City Journal* (Autumn 2000). Accessed online 6 Aug 2012, http://www.city-journal.org/html/issue10_4.html.

wedding but rather a show. When
becoming a man's wife you have to
accept the fact that it's all or nothing. All
the tedious stuff you were doing as a
girlfriend is out the window. Men expect
you to deliver and to bring it. There's
something about marriage that makes life
step up a notch and all kinds of what I
consider unnecessary drama may come in
the beginning, but it's necessary because
it helps develop you in the long run. It
prepares your heart, mind, body, and soul
for the good and bad times. Marriages
have a way of inviting evil, illness, and
death. It's widely believed that marriage is
every woman's dream and that may very
well be so, but I can assure you it can be
a nightmare as well.

When we take vows we know there's a
possibility that anything can happen. There
are no guarantees to marriage. The notion
is that life will be fine and a piece of cake
once you're married, but no one talks
about the heartache enough. The cancers,

viruses that lay dormant in our very existence as humans. The pain that none of us can escape. Death. So be careful what you ask for because, believe me, it can and will happen. However, on somewhat of a lighter note, you should be very happy that a man wants to marry you and join with you until death do you part. That's a very special privilege. Throughout that journey, which may include children, the family bonds will be a blessing.

I heard that life is unfair. Is it really? Why? Because something bad happened to you or a family member, and all of a sudden life seems unfair. The unfair balance comes from you not accepting the fact that things happen and if just for a little bit you resist life, things will become more difficult. You have to learn to embrace change and dance with it. If you're a girlfriend embrace that while you can; I mean don't stay one forever but know that marriage is real and it's a special honor to be considered a man's wife and that it has a lot of responsibility because you're able to create life. This is your likelihood, this is a name that will change life. I'm not sure who's reading this. Maybe you're the First Lady's sister or cousin, or maybe you're the girlfriend of a popular politician. The same rules apply. In relationships there's always going to be an unfair balance. I'm not sure you can do much to change it. Men and women expect things and often we are disappointed. I think the biggest part is to be aware that you're not being mistreated, used, and taken advantage of as a woman, or him as a man. Just because life has its unfair side doesn't mean we as people have to be unfair to one another— especially in relationships. Learn to find an equal balance in your relationship and do your best to be supportive while living the life that best fits you.

Chapter 6

Clocking Out

Sure after a relationship is over a girlfriend may cry, but she can always walk away with all bindings from her relationship free and all chains broken. Alas, for a wife it seems she is more likely to spiral down into an abyss of depression, stemming from the disbelief of an end to death-do-us-part, and possibly financial problems, and a broken family. Even after the fact, a wife is more likely to continue dealing with the remnants of a relationship, bound by the invisible chains of a past commitment.

Manziaflo~

I'm going through a divorce and I've already settled myself emotionally, but how do I deal with the property claims and finances? Why is it this way?

Packadoug

This is what happens when you get married. Stay free while you can. Girlfriends are as free as the wind.

FillaMillet

When I broke up with my boyfriend I was able to just pack my bags and leave. XD

MilleFuelle

Don't get discouraged, this is what happens when you sever a life in two lives that were once joined together.

Girlfriends can live in a separate house without having to split bills, take on his name, or even integrate with his family. Yes, in cohabitation you can split bills, but can it really compare to splitting up everything like in marriage?

Wives have to split most things with their spouse. They live with their spouses, and taking on their name is customary. Being a wife means being a part of his family also, overall, it really is a full-time job.

Girlfriends have the freeing option of leaving a relationship usually with no legal bindings. Wives don't have that readily available freedom. In some places a wife leaving a marriage is the great taboo. Sometimes even if her husband is dead.

A practice called *sati* in India involves the burning (or in some cases burying) of a widow in honor and loyalty to her husband. Usually the widow is dressed in fine clothes, sometimes that which was worn on the wedding day. It is a varying practice and sometimes there is no actual death of the widow at all, rather a symbolic sati. Culture really does matter.

For instance if you look closely in the Bible, if a spouse divorces on any other grounds than adultery, then they are considered adulterers themselves, as is any other person who lies with them.

As you can see, it can be very difficult for a wife to cut her ropes. Especially when it's a fortified rope.

Now let's take a step into the girlfriend's world. What consequences of ending a relationship does a girlfriend really face? Hardly any except for a ticket to a lonely heart. Unless there is a child involved, but there usually isn't. She may have felt as if he was the one, he was using her, or even that it could've never worked. And you know what happens afterwards? She heals, it's not like it was a relationship set in stone and vowed.

But if being a wife is what you want, then so be it. Learn how to step out of your own way. Work well with others. Reduce all selfishness. Stop thinking that life is unfair and that every man owes you something. Always think along the lines of *Well if he can do it so can I, but if he's my man I don't have to be in this alone.*

As I reflect over this book. I had originally thought that a relationship was a job description in itself, but I was wrong. It's life that's a job. We have hundreds if not thousands of challenges to meet daily and of course most of us didn't sign up for the life we have, so instead we embrace as much change as possible.

I hope that you take from this book that if you are alone, you need to focus on yourself in the meantime. Stop trying to make every man your man and stop letting every man tell you he's your man. It's a lot of responsibility to be a man in today's world, no matter what color they are, and for a woman it's hard enough to face the daily task of coping with your own emotions without any man being involved.

Time is very precious and I know we want to spend it with someone that we think we might be in love with. Take your time. Enjoy your life as much as possible. Making that choice to accept a man as your spouse is a decision that needs to be thought out. I hope that you make the right decisions throughout life and I hope that you take the advice I'm giving as a gift of hope, love, and faith that all you need will come in its own perfect time. Girlfriends and wives will be around for a long time. Which side of the fence do you really want to be on when it's all said and done? At some point in life you will be one or the other.

And no sneaking under the fence either. Don't be the girlfriend that's messing with a man while he has a wife. Not a classy look, and as a matter fact you're endangering your own life. I know I'm coming at you raw and a little off topic but if I don't tell you how it is I won't be doing my job. *Girlfriend vs. Wife,* those are the options not the opposing sides. Respect yourself and respect another woman's family.

This book is to help guide you through life so you can make the tough decisions. Men will be around for a very long time and one thing I know for sure is that not every man you see is the man for you. Don't go falling for every man you see that looks nice and dresses well. Some men have some very nasty ways and their habits are unbearable to deal with. Therefore clocking out after a long day's work and going home to a good man is important. I can't express what it feels like to have your own man, someone you can call your own, and to know that he is. Through life, many women will always try to take your man because he's treating you as if you're the last woman standing. Hold on tight because the road will get rough. Just remember what job you applied for and know that all the details of the job description are not listed. Life has its own way of throwing lessons and indescribable events your way. Take life as it comes and please know whatever type of woman you are, you have a duty as a woman to whatever man you commit to. So stop being so defensive about the word "duty." I can't tell you how much it bothers me to hear another women say she doesn't have any duties. No man wants to just take care of you while you sit on your ass all day, and if he does there's something wrong with him. Well, it's time for me to get back to work, I have a lot to finish. It was nice talking with you, hope we can do it again soon..

Do, or do not. There is no "try."

Dmac Poetry House LLC.

Books

Do You Mind if...170,000 sold?
A True Poet Unknown Until Now
I will find my way home
Say Hello to Me
You Can Trust Me
Distance to Love Ratio
Words I never said
Lost in Love
Kamra Sutra without Sex

Girlfriend vs. Wife Duties

www.ingramcontent.com/pod-product-compliance
Lightning Source LLC
LaVergne TN
LVHW011338080426
835513LV00006B/421